Dedication

My daughters Mikayla and Julie are "Pattern Pioneers" who, from the time they were little would say "why do we have to do it THAT way?" Back in those days I would respond "Because that is the way we have always done it!" (I had a LOT to learn!). When they became teenagers I became a student learning from them as they each heard their own call and went on their specific unique adventures. Now it is amazing watching as they use the elixir they discovered in their own delightful ways to make the world a better place.

Acknowledgments

Many of the women leaders who have graced our programs are an integral part of this book. They have all said "there has to be a better way" and each has heard the call to make a difference. Some have challenged their business organizations to start new programs for the younger women leaders. Others have gone into the community to help girls find their voices. Many have learned to tell the truth when in the past they would have preferred to remain silent. A few simply took a deep breath and jumped off the proverbial cliff to leave a job that was unhealthy before finding a new one. There are those who have gone on our adventure journeys with us to Peru and Brazil searching for new ways to solve old problems. I would like to give a shout out to some who have been on major parts of the journey with me: Denise Fantuzzi, Kathleen Belknap, Lynn Rolston, Arezo Hafezi, Marylynn Sauro, Whitney Blackwell, Nancy Singer, Maria Ginnetti, Elaine Sterling, Homeira Carroll, and Debra Neill. You have all made me more courageous watching your courage.

Table of Contents

Introduction

Do you see yourself as a heroine? Never mind! YOU ARE A HEROINE!

Just by wanting to read this book you know you are ready for the adventure. You can look in the mirror and see beyond the obvious. You want to make your mark on the world, yet not really sure what that is, or how to do it. Or you have made your mark and are wondering what is next (hint: there is always a next).

As you read this see what resonates with you. What "tickles your fancy"? That is an old fashioned way to say "what stirs your intuition", or "what floats your boat", or "what really matters to you." When you read pay attention to your GUT, you know, that is a place where GUTSY feelings reside. Listen to your body, it will guide you. Feel those feelings of awakening, of wanting to be someone unique and special. Wanting to do something that will make a difference.

This is YOUR time, use it well.

The Heroine's Journey has three main aspects. It is what classical theater is based upon. There are three acts that build up to a powerful resolution. And guess what? In this heroine's journey YOU are the main character. We will cover each act with some stories of others who have walked this path and transformed their patterns; others who have learned to take the bitter and make it better.

The heroine's journey, in some respects, is like the kids game of "Hide and Seek." Often what you want to find is not initially obvious. You have to check around and get creative, figuring out where WHAT you want is hiding.

So, take off the blinders and yell out to the world *"READY OR NOT HERE I COME!"*

THE 21ST CENTURY GUTSY HEROINE'S JOURNEY

How to Transform Chaos and Conflict to Calmness and Collaboration

SYLVIA LAFAIR

Disclaimers

No patent liability is assumed with respect to the use of the information contained herein.

Although every precaution has been taken in the preparation of this book, the publisher and author assume no responsibility for errors or omissions.

Neither is any liability assumed for damages resulting from the use of the information contained herein.

While all the stories are true, the names and companies have been changed to protect the privacy of the individuals.

Copyright © November 2014
ISBN 978-0-9883625-6-7

Printed in the United States of America
Published November 2014

creative energy options
CEO
PUBLISHING

45 Country Place Lane
White Haven, PA 18661
570.636.3858
sylvia@ceoptions.com
www.ceoptions.com

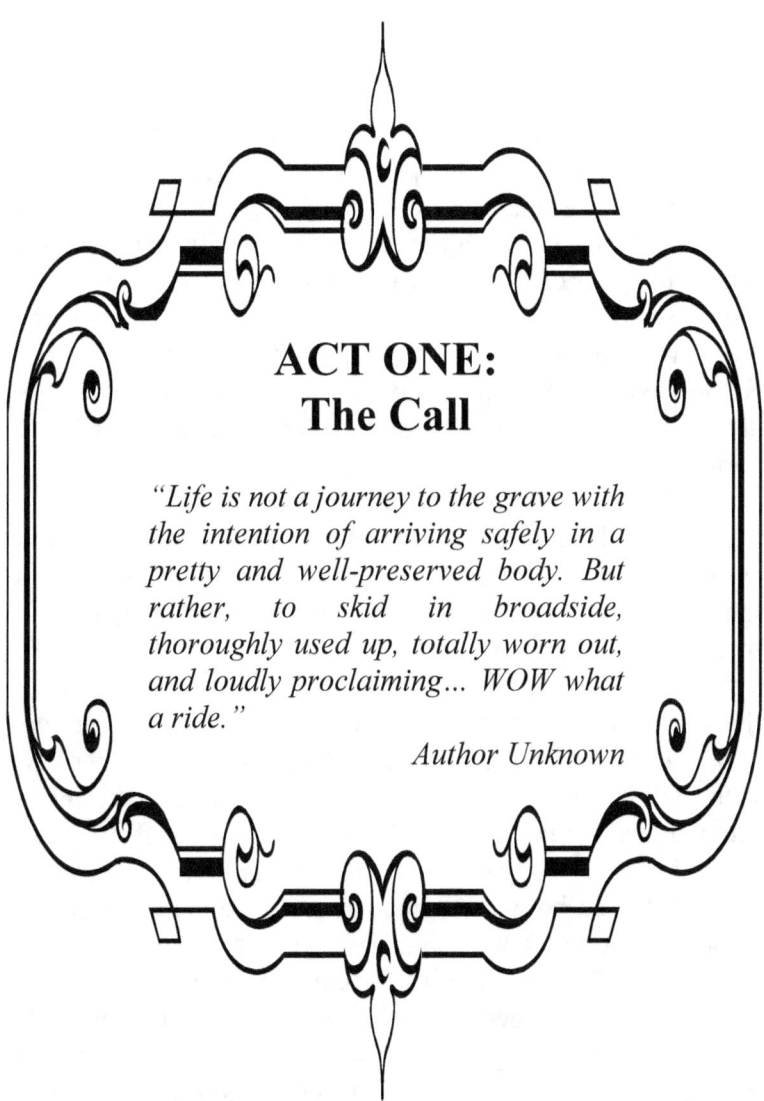

ACT ONE:
The Call

"Life is not a journey to the grave with the intention of arriving safely in a pretty and well-preserved body. But rather, to skid in broadside, thoroughly used up, totally worn out, and loudly proclaiming... WOW what a ride."

Author Unknown

The Call: It is like a knock on the door or a whack on the side of the head. Something happens when you least expect it. Or you get to the place where you say, "never again." A relationship turns sour, a job disappears, health issues arise, a family member dies, a big wind topples a tree on your house, the rains won't stop and floods force you to evacuate the area. You have a fight with your sister, you find out that your best friend is spreading rumors about you behind your back, you are passed over for the promotion that you knew had your name on it.

No one is immune to this knock. No one, ever.

I will take you on the Heroine's Journey with four flesh and blood women who live right here and right now in the 21st century, facing what we all face, the challenges of making a life that works.

We will also briefly discuss Princess Psyche who is the star of the oldest recorded myth of all time *"Psyche and Eros."* Only we will see her through the eyes of a modern girl who finds her own "Princessness" and shows all girls growing into women that it is possible to face fear and transform it into GUTSINESS. I suggest you check out "Princess Charm School" to see how contemporary girls are being taught the basics of courage and facing obstacles. In the past it would have been "The Wizard of Oz." More on this in a minute.

Back to Princess Psyche. She had to go through the journey to gain strength and become worthy of the royal title. Young girls of today, thanks to films and stories that "tickle their fancy" are learning that the title of Princess only comes with the same three major events in life: the call, initiation, and return.

Almost all little girls today go through a princess phase. Just look around at any airport and little girls under the age of seven are wearing frilly little tutus or pink t-shirts and pink ballet shoes. They are all signed up to be part of Team Princess. I talk about that in my book "GUTSY: How Women Leaders Make Change." You can get a copy of this award winning book on Amazon. In there I look at some of the forces that have formed us from birth through adulthood. And you can read a great interpretation of the full story of *Psyche and Eros*.

This ancient myth is at the core of understanding feminine psychology and is still very vital for modern women today, as well as for men, to understand the softer aspects of their own nature. You see, we all have both the strong and the soft sides of our lives. We all can be daring and caring. When there is balance between the masculine and feminine in our natures we can move to a world where we can all share the richness of life. No longer needing to stay in the tight box of "should" and "have-to" we can have a more healthy equation of daring plus caring to equal sharing.

Sharing. Good idea whose time has come. Sharing. Both the finances and the family. Sharing. For better or for worse. Sharing. That is what the world needs and we all want more of. Sharing.

DARING + CARING = SHARING

However, until women become strong and daring there is limited balance in the world. Once women can gain strength to find their own resources to handle tough situations men can heave a big sigh, relax, and let their caring side out.

"Wait" you say "Why do we have to become daring before men can become caring? That is just not right!"

And you have a point there. However, YOU are the one reading this now so YOU can make the change that will lead to other's making equally wonderful changes.

You see, we do impact and change each other. We really do! Yet, it has to start somewhere and why not let it start with you. Try on a daring adventure for size. I promise it will not just change you, it will change the world around you.

Now, back to the myth of *Psyche and Eros*. It shows up everywhere. I was surprised at how pervasive it is even now in this century of fast technology, fast cars, and fast thinking. All the components of the heroine's journey, the call, initiation, and return are still here. No, you cannot skip one of the three main phases of growth and development. The call to adventure is in all of us, it is there for young and old. It is, to put it simply, what happens when you live life fully.

Even little girls become aware of the journey thanks to that ever present force in our culture, Barbie. You know Barbie, that doll who makes her appearance generation after generation. Even Barbie has morphed from a simple plastic doll into an action gal who can fight for what she believes.

I was with my nine year old granddaughter who cajoled me into watching a Barbie inspired movie with her. Initially I felt frustrated. A granddaughter of mine watching a Barbie movie. I would not ever buy Barbie dolls for her mother when she was a child. I saw them as sexist and limiting for little girls to become the best they could be.

As they were growing up I did not want my daughters to think that the path to a joyful life was being super thin, having long straight hair and spending time worrying about clothes and shoes. And decades ago Barbie was simply there to dress to impress her boyfriend Ken.

Not anymore.

Here I was with Arielle watching "Princess Charm School." At first all my old judgments came flooding back and then I settled in to watch this bit of fluff. Soon I heard myself saying aloud, "I cannot believe it. This is a modern heroine's journey." And my granddaughter said "Sure it is grand mom, whatever that means." The story is not that different from what Psyche had to go through to become strong and really gain the title of princess.

It began with a most unlikely girl winning the lottery to go to Princess Charm School at the castle. She had to leave her job as a waitress and compete with others to get her tiara. And once she gets there, after resisting the call she has a series of initiations to become strong, competent, and confident. After facing fears, standing up for oneself, and doing the right thing, the heroine becomes a strong, new improved version of herself.

Curious, I asked my granddaughter what she learned from watching the movie. Her response was wonderful. "I think that she was afraid and didn't think anyone would like her because she was from a poor family. I think that once she learned to be strong and not sit in a corner and sulk people started to like her. And, grand mom, she was lucky to have a little fairy like Tinker Bell help her with everything."

At the end of the film it becomes clear that every girl can become a princess. It is all about courage and creativity. It's about having help from friends, not letting enemies get you down, and listening to the forces in the invisible world help. Let's hear it for all the Tinker Bells. Let's hear it for Barbie!!

The following four stories, all true I might add, show that in each personal story there is a universal one. Parts of each story will resonate with you. You see, the heroine's journey is one we all take. No wait…. Let me change that. The heroine's journey is one that we are all offered. There is ALWAYS that initial knock on the door. Some open the door at once, others ignore that knock year after year. Some who simply cannot take that first fierce step only answer the knock at the moment of crisis. Others of us end our days steeped in regret for the paths not taken.

You are here, reading this which means you are ready. Pay attention and you can have a life of vitality where you feel engaged, connected, and totally alive!

The knock of the call says "What you have learned until now is not enough. There is more than repeating and repeating the behavior patterns of the past. Open the door and come into new territory to rediscover parts of yourself, parts of your story that have been buried in the hidden folds of your memory."

Being GUTSY means facing the fear of the unknown and learning how to make change happen. Always remember that there are outer and inner forces to help. When we run out of ideas on what to do fate has a way of stepping in. Listen with your ears, with your mind, and with your heart.

Join the following women who have all been coaching clients of mine and have been through the GUTSY WOMEN WEEKEND program. Think about your own challenges, your own decisions, your own willingness or reticence to take that leap from now to new.

What is interesting with the four you are about to meet is that at work you would never suspect some of the tough times they have encountered. We mostly wear our professional faces at work and rarely show the conflicts and struggles that have preceded us or are going on the minute we go home.

Now I am not suggesting we do a "tell all" at work. What I am suggesting is that as you move into your strength as a leader you pay attention to the fact that there are whole human beings behind the title of marketing director, or administrative assistant, or internet developer.

The woman who waits on you in Nordstrom's has a story and may be in the middle of her initiation phase. The woman who sits next to you at the leadership conference may have just heard the call and is getting ready to leave her job and start her own business out of boredom or frustration.

The real estate agent who coos over the beautiful house she spotted for your move may be the one to share her wisdom with you from her own life lessons. Ya neveh know!

In each of the following stories is a woman who chose or was forced to make changes. She had to contend with the forces of family (believe me this is a strong pull) culture (often even a stronger pull) and crises (that can exhaust even the bravest person).

The circumstances are unique to each individual and yet, we can all imagine abuse that is often verbal, perhaps physical, and sadly also for some, sexual. We all know that sense of separation. That first sense of separation came when the umbilical cord was cut and there we were naked and crying. There are the great themes of life that have to do with abandonment, betrayal, and what happens if we risk speaking out in a world that tells us to be good, behave, and be quiet.

The following stories belong to the four individual women and yet, they also belong to all of us. Let us follow them as they hear the call.

Patricia Hears the Call

As a little girl Patricia was always too afraid to tell anyone that her father beat her mother. She went to school and was both mum and numb. The hitting went on for years. She begged her mother to get help. Her mother simply shook her head and put her finger to her lips for them both to be quiet. Her mother taught her daughter to be silent, invisible. She modeled her mother's behavior and stayed in the shadows.

In her early twenties she married only to repeat the pattern. She thought she was getting out of a horrible home only to create a variation on the theme from her childhood. She married a man who began to beat her. She was invisible to the world and to herself.

She had a job as an executive assistant. She was smart and fast. She was a self-starter. However, she still hid from the world. That is, until that day when the knock came on the door, the knock that said "It is your time. Get ready to start on the path. Some of the time it will be scary and sometimes full of laughter. The good news is you will move from invisible to become GUTSY." How she learned to be seen and heard is the tale of transformation we will discuss.

What did she do?

One last slap across the face leaving her with a bleeding lip was it. She took her young son and left. She left a note and moved in with a high school girl friend who helped her start her life anew.

She went to her boss, a kind man and asked for more responsibility. Soon she was promoted.

The departure, the call to adventure, the time for real and lasting change was finally here. She would no longer be an avoider like her mother. It was the last time she ever, ever permitted a man to raise a hand to hurt her. It was the last time she was willing to be like her mother and deny what was going on.

Her husband came to her pleading for reconciliation. She knew if she went back before he looked at his behavior, before she really did a deep dive to understand why she had stayed so long, why she was willing to pretend all was good when it wasn't, they would soon repeat the pattern. First, she had to learn what it means to be GUTSY.

Emma Hears the Call

She was the rebel in the family. Not the way you think. She was not the one who got bad grades or created havoc by staying out late of smoking cigarettes behind the tress in the back yard. Instead she became a parent to her parents. The pot smoking and then cocaine in her home was over the top. When, as a young teen, she complained to her parents and older siblings that it was not good for them they laughed and told her to either join them or be quiet.

Emma lived in a "proper" middle class neighborhood and everyone she knew smoked. First cigarettes and then marijuana at one time or another. Yet, only in her house were the adults worse than the kids.

Eventually Emma left. She dropped out of high school and went to live with her aunt. She worked at a local hotel cleaning rooms. At age seventeen some "kindly man" took her into his motel room. They had, as she described it, consensual sex, and he sent her on her way. Too inexperienced she was one of those "one in a million" girls who ended up pregnant. Afraid she would lose her job she never told anyone. She was a big girl and strong. So until the baby bump became too prominent she continued to clean rooms, feeling alone and afraid.

As her belly grew she made a fateful decision to give the child up for adoption. A local charity took her in and after a little girl was safely born and sent to an adoptive home, Emma started counseling to figure out her life. She eventually went to school and became an accountant, working days and going to night school.

All grown up Emma had an excellent job. She became head of the tax department in a well-respected company. No one would have ever thought she came from such a difficult family and had so many dark secrets. However, she still had

16

an unrelenting sense of being a victim. And the sense of shame kept her tied in knots, especially the knot of "not being good enough."

The knock did not come for Emma when she left home. It did not come when she gave the baby up for adoption. The knock came when she was diagnosed with breast cancer and had to go through that awful initiation called chemotherapy. Now was the time to totally give up the victim mentality and show what she was really made of.

Carole Hears the Call

Carole had some great ideas on how to make her family home more functional. As the second oldest of seven children, she watched her mother work herself to exhaustion. She felt the need to help her mother keep up with the load of housework, to make it faster and easier. So, she created new and better ways to sort and fold.

Carole did the sorting and then the folding and then the dusting and then the vacuuming and then the dishes and then the food preparation. She was so good that soon she was in the role of the over-giving, martyr. Everyone came to her to do this and that and solve all the problems of the day. She felt suffocated and feared she would never get free, yet she did everything for everyone and could have won the crown for martyr of the year. She stayed home, went to a local college, and graduated with a degree in education. She taught first grade where there were still constant demands of her emotionally.

A pretty woman, Carole met an amazing man and just like the story books she loved to read to her first grade class. They married and were to live happily ever after. Until that knock came at her door. It was in the form of a friend telling her that her husband of eight years and one child later was cheating on her with a neighbor who lived a few houses away.

At first she ignored what had been said. It was just gossip she told herself. Until the night she saw a couple who looked like they were very much in love holding hands walking through the mall and she could no longer avoid facing the betrayal only yards in front of her. The pattern of over-giving and pleasing to keep the peace was about to explode her life into new and eventually remarkable ways.

At the moment Carole could only lick the wounds of the hurt and betrayal. However, soon she was going to transform the pleaser inside of her into a powerful and clear truth teller.

Samantha Hears the Call

Finally there is Samantha. She grew up in a wealthy family where there were vacations to beautiful resorts, private school, parties and fun. Except, what was demanded in return for her great life was perfection. She was a "trophy child" who was told to watch every extra pound of weight, exercise every day, make sure her grades were all A's, and date only the top guys at school. She was seen as strong, a gal who had all the answers.

Her peers all wanted to be just like her. Yet, perfect had its downside. She slept poorly and had constant stomach aches. She had no one to tell her despair to. She had it all. It would be selfish to complain. After college she went with a top consulting firm and rose through the ranks at warp speed. She was the super achiever and had a bright red lipstick smile painted on her face. She was a super achiever to the max. No place for mistakes, for being wrong, ever.

There was no room for vulnerability. Until that knock came on her door to say she had a choice to learn about being vulnerable or find herself very, very sick. Disbelieving she closed the door. However, six months later the knock was too loud to ignore and she also started on her journey.

Depression is a funny thing. No, I do not mean depression is funny. I mean that no one really knows how the physical, mental, and emotional weave together to make someone slump to the sidelines of life and wonder if it is all worth it.

Samantha thought about taking her own life. She began to hide the meds she was taking and store them for a night when she could swallow all of them at once, knowing her body would have to shut down and she could hopefully find peace in a place that did not demand perfection.

She woke up staring into the eyes of her distraught boyfriend. She was gaunt and worn, no make-up to hide the sadness and fear. Her perfection had melted away and she was just a frail body wrapped in a medical gown with hair hanging limply past her shoulders. Yet, she could hear that inner voice saying to her "Welcome to the adventure."

YOUR TURN:

NOW Ms. HEROINE, it is your turn: Think of what is going on in your life right now. What are the positives and what are the challenges. What are the patterns you have been handed by your family and your culture? What brings you joy? What makes you want to get in bed and put the covers over your head?

_____

_____

_____

_____

Think big and bold. You can do it. Take the leap of faith and look into your life. If you look you can open the door to the call, you can plan your own next step. Otherwise it will sneak up on you when you are not really ready. Take charge, get GUTSY!

The modern heroine is not sitting on the sidelines, she hears the call to departure on her own terms. That is part of what makes today's heroines unique and powerful.

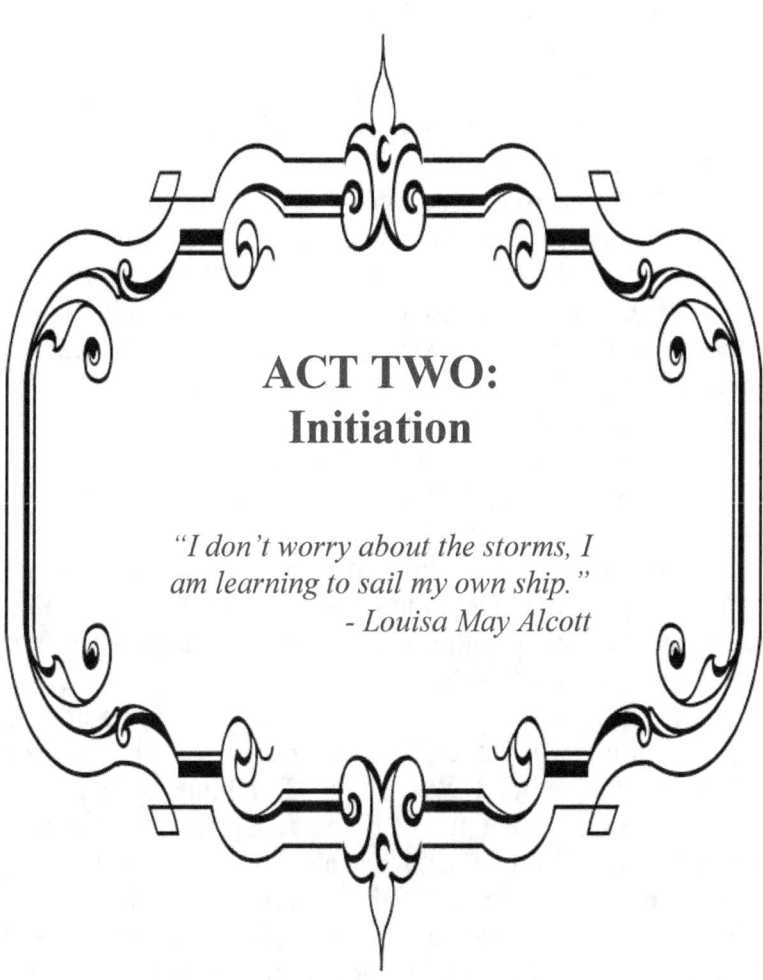

ACT TWO:
Initiation

*"I don't worry about the storms, I
am learning to sail my own ship."*
- Louisa May Alcott

Initiation: Today's heroine says "There are many ways to get to the top of the mountain." Not willing to be typecast or put into a very tight container, modern heroines stand up straight and say "I will decide what is right, what matters in my life. I will not let my mother, or father, or siblings, or culture or friends tell me how to live my life."

As the heroine goes into the initiation phase she is clearer than in past generations and is more willing to take the leaps of faith needed to move beyond the fear and anger of the past. There is a willingness to see through the obvious. There is a desire to forgive. However, forgiveness is not a blanket statement of "all is forgiven." Forgiveness comes after the work of looking at another individual's life and understanding the pushes and pulls of their mean-spirited behavior.

Forgiveness is about creating new, positive boundaries and sticking with it without making excuses.

Initiation means being open to outcome, not attached to it. It means looking into the shadows at the sides and seeing that ugly witch/bitch within and learning to transform it. (Hint: we All have this ugly side).

During the initiation phase the heroine learns how to tell the truth without denial or indulgence. The deepest learning is that telling the truth is NOT spilling your guts.

During initiations it becomes apparent that outer nature, sitting beside a stream, watching the sun fall over a mountain, looking at small fish in a pond, watching flowers blowing in the breeze, all have a place for growth and learning. Outer nature is a path to our inner nature.

During this phase there is powerful comprehension that family is the first and most powerful grouping that will show up in many ways for the rest of life and needs to be considered seriously.

There is a quote from famed psychiatrist Carl Jung that is vital in the initiation phase:

> *I feel very strongly that I am under the influence of things or questions which were left incomplete and unanswered by my parents and grandparents and more distant ancestors. It often seems as if there were an impersonal karma within a family which is passed on from parents to children. It has always seemed to me that I had to answer questions which fate had posed to my forefathers, and which had not yet been answered, or as if I had to complete, or perhaps continue, things which previous ages had left unfinished." (Memories, Dreams, and Reflections).*

Taking all these ideas into consideration let's look at some of the initiations from our four modern day heroines.

Patricia's Initiations

Patricia set up a meeting with her estranged husband. She had spent time learning about how patterns repeat and repeat and she wanted her husband, the father of her child to see his part in continuing the abuse that had become a learned behavior when they were both children.

They went out to dinner. He seemed willing to do anything to get her back, to have "business as usual."

However, when she tip-toed into the reasons for the abuse, the smacks and slaps, he became belligerent and blamed her "big mouth" for all the problems.

The evening ended on a sour note and she once again found herself retreating to the realm of invisibility.

"I learned nothing" she wailed to the wind on the way home. I am just a weak-willed loser.

Then at work the next day she leaned that there would be an office reorganization and she would now report to the woman she disliked the most at work. Feeling she had no options she accepted her fate and went home early with a major headache.

Two strikes in two days. And then fate stepped in. Her husband came to take their young son to sleep overnight. She told him she was disappointed and frustrated. He shouted that she was to blame. Normally at this point she would glide into the other room while he took their son. She was rendered once again invisible.

Yet, one last nasty word was sent her way and she flew into action. She grabbed him by the sleeve and as he lost balance she pushed him into a chair. Then standing over him she let out all the rage that had built up for years. It was a controlled rage. Her voice was deep and strong. Her sentences were short and left no room for interpretation.

It was the alignment of head, and heart that made him sit and listen. She had finally thrown off the invisible cloak and spoke her truth from a place deep within. Possibly, as Jung said, she was talking for all the women, all the ancestors who for generations had stood quiet while their stomachs were in a whirl.

For the first time she knew what the word daring really meant and felt like. It was another turning point to move to a life of creativity and joy.

Emma's Initiations

Until now, the "C" word had always been a degrading word for a female. She had even called other women a "cunt" at times.

Now, however, that was simply a boring slang word. The real "C" word meant life or death.

Emma had that haunting feeling that if she were to die she would have left undone the always dreamt of meeting with her birth daughter. Now, not knowing what was ahead she decided that time had collapsed and she was a woman in a hurry.

Modern technology was a gift. She searched and found her daughter while tooling around the internet. She began to follow her as best she could, learning her name was Martha, a name she hated. However, the daughter was now turning twenty and, oh my God, did she resemble her long forgotten mother. It was as if she was looking at a younger version of herself.

"I have no time to go half way across the country to meet her. And what if she rejects me?"

These were her daily thoughts and yet, she would continue to find ways to follow her daughter's life story.

Again fate intervened.

At a company dinner Emma had too much to drink and started to flirt with some of the best customers that while she had known for years were still personal strangers to her. She poked in the ribs to get a laugh, she pulled on neckties to get attention, and she even went to pick up her boss as they were going to get yet another drink.

"Emma, I think you have had enough alcohol." He said as he pulled away. He knew she would start chemotherapy in a few weeks and was concerned for her. She was still strong and larger than this very proper man and she went to pick him up anyway. That was the end of a career. Sometimes a moment is all that is needed for life to change.

The next week she knew when the H.R. representative came to visit her on a sultry summer afternoon and that she was given an extended leave of absence. Now, before her treatment started she had time to think, to ponder the future.

Day after day she wondered why she had sabotaged her success. She would play that fateful night over and over in her head.

Then she made a big decision. She would meet her birth daughter.

Emma sent an email and the girl responded. Initially it was what she expected. "Do not, under any circumstances, bother me."

In a coaching session I prodded her to go slowly yet, keep going.

Emails followed, all with the same response. Until Emma texted that she was driving half way across the country for the chance to meet her daughter face to face.

Her daughter texted back that she was not ready to meet this woman who had given her away so many years ago. Emma knew from our work that she was in the initiation phase and made a decision to keep going. She would go to the motel and call her daughter and let fate decide what was next. However, she would not run away, not go back to her old pattern of leaving when the going gets tough.

"We did meet" she said in an elated tone. Not only did we meet we went out to dinner and I met her boyfriend of two years. The next day we both talked for hours and my birth daughter hugged me and said that I had filled a hole she had lived with for all of her twenty-one years. It was magic,"

And then after a very quiet few minutes she said "You know Sylvia, if I had not lost my job I would not ever have taken the time for this trip. Now I am ready to face the world in a new way and I just know I will beat the cancer."

Carole's Initiations

"Why do I always think of myself last?" Carole said as she dropped into the sofa in my office. "Why did I pick being an elementary school teacher where there are always needy kids who can suck you dry? Why did I pick a man who is so narcissistic that all he ever did was take and take from me and then run off with another woman and lie about it to boot?"

Good questions that Carole had to face in her time of initiation.

First was to talk with the man she had married for better or for worse and now was stuck in that for worse place.

She did not want a divorce. She wanted to work it out. But how? Again, fate showed her the way. She was forced to stand and be counted.

Her husband was doing the typical affair thing, calling her and saying he was working late. She wanted to believe him and yet she knew he was lying through his teeth. As she sat by the window waiting for him to come home she began to doze off. It was almost midnight and yet she was not willing to get in bed. Suddenly she felt as if she someone had kicked her in the shins. She sat straight up and, as she told me, heard a voice say in a neutral tone, "Go to his office."

She ignored the voice in her head and began to doze once more. Then a loud sound awakened her once again. It was a neighbor putting out the garbage and trash cans were banging and bumping along the cement to the street.

That voice again neutral and clear telling her to get in the car and go to his office.

This time she paid attention. Her accountant husband had an office only blocks away and when she got there and saw the dim lights from the reception room she froze. Ready to turn back, to stay the good girl, the pleaser, she stood near her car until she saw a man and a woman walk out the door.

And there she was face to face with her husband and another woman.

As she tells it she became electric. Every part of her was alive and ready and after her first "Well hello you two" she could not be contained. She was eloquent in her choice of words, proud of her actions and how she talked with both of them about the betrayal.

Suffering does not make a good story, neither is suffering an initiation. Truth makes a good story and it is only through truth that we are initiated.

Carole stood there in that eternal triangle and told her husband she was not willing to throw their marriage to the winds. She wanted them to find a way to get through this mess and be together. She told "the other woman" to get a grip and find out why she needed another woman's husband, why she needed to slink in the dark of the night, and to look inside to see what she was afraid of.

And then she turned, got in her car and told her husband they could continue this at home. She left, not knowing what would happen. She knew, she told me, that whatever came from this the truth had set her free.

Samantha's Initiations

Her decision was not to go on medication. She decided it would dull her sense and she needed to find out where that damn depression was lodged in her body and mind.

So, Samantha took a leave of absence for what she called a "radical sabbatical" and went to live in a village in Peru. Not just any village, a very, very basic village where she slept on a mat on a dirt floor and when it was hot she fanned herself with a newspaper.

She was there to teach the youngsters English and bone up on her Spanish. She was there to help with the daily chores and sit at night looking at the stars truly like diamonds in the sky. She had time to think.

There were not many mirrors in the village and Samantha pulled her hair into an unfashionable pony tail and wore cotton dresses that had no sex appeal, no style, just covering for a body. Her only make-up was the sunscreen to protect her from the hot afternoon sun.

Samantha watched how the mothers talked to the children. It was soft and sweet. She watched the kids play from morning till dark other than for her English lessons. It was summer and time to explore, adventure, and wonder.

Samantha began to unwind. Her super achiever personality began to dull and another side of her started to peek through.

She stopped looking for perfection and instead started to accept each day for whatever was shown to her.

And then one day a beautiful little girl, the Peruvian children are truly gorgeous, came to sit with her and in halting English asked her if she had children and what they were like. A few sentences later Samantha began to cry. For no reason.

The little girl ran to get her a cloth to dry her face and then just sat next to her and held her hand.

Samantha knew she would soon return to the States and reclaim her job. Yet, she also knew that all the designer labels would be meaningless and she would never again care so much about the symbol of success that was on whatever car she would drive.

A letter started to take shape in her mind. It was a letter to her parents telling them to throw all the trophies away, they were meaningless. What was meaningful was holding hands with that little Peruvian village girl who would follow Samantha everywhere.

Her radical sabbatical worked. It was the best medicine she could have ever taken. And when she went back to her apartment, to her job she was also radical. She started to talk to her direct reports and ask them about who they are, what really matters to them. Initially word was out that "SAMANTHA has gone California."

Many of her friends began to shy away, could not relate. They joked and asked her what she was smoking. Soon she found that she was as frustrated with her peers as they were with her.

She went to talk with her parents. She wanted to know them as people, not just two older people who dressed well and went to fancy restaurants. She asked them about their childhoods. They were uncomfortable did not have a clue why she was asking.

There was a period of utter loneliness until a new wave of friends began to fill the void. They understood how a suicide attempt could be turned into the call to adventure. They also talked about their tests and trials and Samantha began to let the new world in.

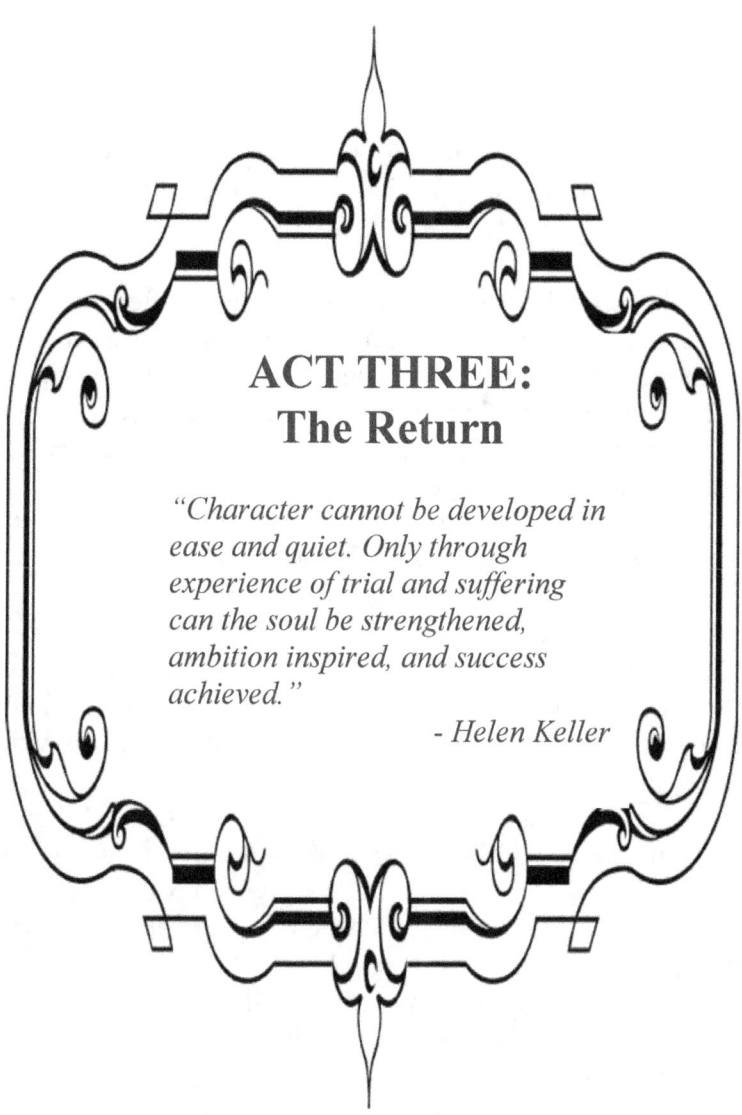

ACT THREE:
The Return

"Character cannot be developed in ease and quiet. Only through experience of trial and suffering can the soul be strengthened, ambition inspired, and success achieved."

- Helen Keller

The Return: The return has elements of a purifying ritual. You come back from all the inner and outer tests refreshed and able to see what you could never see before.

T.S. Eliot's poem says it so well:

"We shall never cease from exploration, and the end of all our exploring will be to arrive where we started and know the place for the first time."

The return is a true homecoming. There is often laughter and tears, happy tears. It is a time of celebration. For when a heroine returns she brings with her the elixir that was trapped until she was able to find it and take it with her. The elixir is not a material product. It is the elixir of love, of freedom, of wisdom, and of knowledge.

The change does not have to be dramatic. It can be quiet. It is, however, noticed. Often family members, friends, and colleagues will say "you look different" or "I can't put my finger on it but your voice sounds more resonant" or "you seem to understand what I mean now more than before."

The patterns of behavior that were there for security and survival have been transformed into ones that are fraught with power and caring.

You can get the full list of patterns in the GUTSY book and you can take the pattern aware quiz by going to www.ceoptions.com. Here you can see which patterns would be good for you to transform when you go on your own journey.

The return is where you start to live from a place of wholeness. It is a place where there is more calm, more joy, and more laughter.

The return is where you become irresistible. Not in a seedy seductive way, more in the way that people simply want to hang around with you. You become a teacher. Not in the traditional sense, in the way of being able to listen and help others also see through new eyes. It is rewarding and fun. You now see how everything is connected and that no one wins unless we all do. There is less judgment and more acceptance.

And yet, you will not, nor should you, give your power away. You still stand strong and will tell the truth without judgment, blame or attack. You have a voice that is steady and the pleaser in you is now the truth teller. The avoider pattern is now the initiator who does not run away and will start the tough conversations. The super achiever who was once weighed down striving for perfection is now a creative collaborator who loves to give credit to the team not just oneself.

Let's fast forward two years into the future of the four women who heard the call and began their heroine's journey.

Patricia's Return

Patricia did not get what she thought she wanted. She did however, get what she needed. Her picture of a happy marriage had not, until now, included equality and core sharing. She always thought she would have to be the one to make it all work by constant concessions.

She was divorced from her first husband who was not willing to even look at his part in any conflict. He stayed in a macho place of self-righteousness.

Once Patricia was able to speak her truth without flinching for fear of being hurt, physically or verbally, she was able to close the door of the pattern of generations of women who put their finger up to their lips to remember to be quiet. Those days were over.

It showed up everywhere, this new, improved Patricia. She was promoted several times and was being groomed for a vice president job in the marketing area of her company. She was sought after as a mentor for the newer employees, and was now in a relationship with a man who was willing to meet her half way to make the relationship blossom.

The elixir Patricia shared with all who came into her life: speak out and be heard.

Emma's Return

Emma was now cancer free. And she learned to love the "C' word. It had opened doors to new ways to be in the world. She was vibrant in her physical body, eating only organic foods and mostly fresh fruits and vegetables.

She took her new chance at life and did some clean-up work with her family. This was done by letter writing since every time she went to talk with her parents and siblings they were like stone mountains.

The letters she crafted took time. They were not for publication, however, they were edited and polished so that when they were finally sent to her family she knew she could close the door to the past hurts.

Emma and her birth daughter continue to reach out to each other in small and positive ways. There was a meeting with Emma, the girl, and the adoptive parents so they could feel comfortable with the budding relationship with their daughter.

For Emma, coming from a home where her parents were like children and behaved badly having clear and definite boundaries is vital. She works at this every day.

She returned to work in her new and improved state and like Patricia is a sought after mentor. She is also dating and looking at how she can have a rich and caring relationship where she can hear and be heard.

The elixir brought back by Patricia: Being clear and creating healthy boundaries. This is crucial for all relationships. She loves the paradox that good boundaries give more freedom.

Carole's Return

There was a career change for Carole. While she loved the little children she had guided at the early stage of their school days, she knew she needed something that would not put so many demands on her emotionally, or rather different emotional demands.

She went back to school to become an expert in internet marketing. Working with a small company of energizer bunny folks her days were filled with laughs and ideas that sparkled and promotions that soon became award winners.

At home she was now in the relationship she had desired. It was open, honest, and filled with the juicy fun of sensual and sexual pleasure.

Who was she with? Did you say it was that jerk who cheated on her and lied to her and pretended everything was fine with her when it wasn't? Well, you were right!

She did what is very tough to do. She stepped beyond the betrayal to find out what was really going on at the invisible level. She has to look at both her behavior as well as her husband's and get past blame to honesty and realness.

When Carole could see how her obsessive caretaking behavior was suffocating the marriage, when she could see that she was not able to talk about what she wanted and needed and was always making it just fine for her husband she was on her way to grab the elixir and bring it back for a better life.

Now, don't get mad at her for taking some of the ownership of the ugly affair. She and her husband did some good coaching together and he also was able to talk about his destructive behavior.

They worked at it together and both learned that accountability is worth its weight in gold.

The elixir Carole brought back: Taking ownership of your part in any conflict opens up room for others to come forward and be accountable.

Samantha's Return

Every time Samantha heard herself begin to doubt her work as not good enough she would pinch herself on her left arm. This was her anchor. A slight pinch and she could look in the mirror and say "Hey dummy, remember you can be perfectly imperfect or imperfectly perfect, so which do you choose?"

Her work was always stellar and she still wanted to be the best she could be. However, now she realized that being the best does not always mean you must be first.

Samantha and her boyfriend got married last year and they are now discussing children. Long talks late at night brought forth an agreement that they would love healthy, beautiful children who could be free to explore life by making mistakes and seeing failure as an opportunity.

No trophy kids would ever live in their home.

Samantha also wanted to give back. The time in Peru had healed her. Initially she wanted to go back to Peru and then she realized that there were so many children right in her own city that needed help with better English that she volunteered at an inner city school to teach creative writing to sixth graders.

Samantha's elixir: Being first is exhausting and being best is an inner journey. She teaches this to pre-teens and is soon going to teach this to her own children.

CONCLUSION

There you have it. The knock, the call to adventure, the departure from how you are living life right now is just a heartbeat away.

Pay attention. I suggest you answer the call no matter how inconvenient or frightening.

As a modern heroine your job is to be a model of daring and caring and sharing. You are here to help make the world a better place and please, please remember that "we are all connected and no one wins unless we all do."

Joyous Journeys and much love.

Author's Page

 Sylvia Lafair, PhD has dedicated her career to helping individuals become their best. First as a psychologist working with families and couples and then making a left hand turn into the world of business leadership and team development.

Her "UNIQUE" ideas have had widespread influence in corporations, family firms, and entrepreneurial start-ups.

The past 25 years have been spent helping executives, managers, and teams connect the dots of how personal and professional behavior cannot be separated. She has trained a staff of executive coaches and facilitators in her Pattern Aware™ model.

What has been eye-opening in all manner of organizations is that when stress hits the hot button we all tend to revert to patterns from childhood that were there to keep us safe. While they may have helped at five or seven or twelve, they can run havoc in adult relationships.

Working with companies around the world it became clear that the universal aspects of what it means to be in relationships is not very different regardless of culture, size of company, or product. Everywhere there is the yearning for all of us to get along. Dr. Lafair's innovative work gives us the directives to make this happen.

Her book *'Don't Bring It to Work'* has won nine awards and with its companion *'Pattern Aware Success Guide,'* has been used in graduate programs and by work teams worldwide.

Her book, *'GUTSY: How Women Leaders Make Change'* has also won six book awards and led to her highly successful **GUTSY Women Weekend Retreats**.

This newest book *'UNIQUE: How Story Sparks Diversity, Inclusion and Engagement,'* is based on the powerful model of storytelling called **Sankofa Mapping ™**.

Dr. Lafair's abilities to blend story with fact and humor make her a sought after speaker, workshop facilitator, and executive coach.

Her **Total Leadership Connections Program ™**, now in its fourteenth year, has been named one of the top leadership development programs in 2014 by Leadership Excellence/H.R.com, making this the third year in a row.

Dr. Lafair has been featured in *The Wall Street Journal, Forbes* and *Time* as well as on the *Today Show* with Kathie Lee and Hoda.

For further information or to book Dr. Lafair for a consultation or speaking engagement please call her office at 570.636.3858 or email her directly at sylvia@ceoptions.com.